Who Speaks for Wolf

Who Speaks for Wolf

A NATIVE AMERICAN LEARNING STORY

As Told to Turtle Woman Singing by her father,
Sharp-eyed Hawk

By Paula Underwood Spencer
Art by Frank Howell

Tribe of Two Press • Austin • 1983

Permission to reproduce the paintings and drawings in this book was granted to Paula Underwood Spencer by artist Frank Howell.

This first edition has been made possible by the Meredith Slobod Crist Memorial Fund in Austin, Texas, and by the Overseas Education Fund in Washington, D.C. through funds contributed to them in memory of Meredith Crist. All proceeds from this edition will go to further the purposes of the MSCMF.

Edited by Jeanne Lamar Slobod

Designed by Robert J. Helberg

For information about the Meredith Slobod Crist Memorial Fund write:

    Meredith Fund
    1801 Lavaca #12-K
    Austin, Texas 78701

For information about the book, WHO SPEAKS FOR WOLF, write:

    Tribe of Two Press
    P. O. Box 1763
    Austin, Texas 78767

4

In Memory of Meredith

Bright comet
Briefly seen
Illuminating life
With a glad vision

Acknowledgements

A grateful heart remembers —

How Marianne Karydes always understood.

How Ann Schrogie brought a gift of blank book and said, "Now start writing,"

How Jeanne Lamar Slobod asked to share the task, adding a new dimension to friendship,

How Sonja Elmer turned script into typed pages, always asking for more,

How Jess Wilson Muelken retained a listening ear, delighting in the hearing,

How Meredith Crist expanded the horizons of a sometimes dimming world,

How Jerry Wagner introduced the artists in the creative ambiance of Santa Fe,

How Frank Howell concluded, "We say the same things through two different media,"

How Robert Louis Slobod decided, "We can do it, but let's do it one step at a time,"

How Charles and Mary Lou Holt asked to be a part,

How Bob Helberg fitted the pieces into a delightful whole,

How very dear friends are.

But most of all a grateful heart remembers —

The kind and loving support of Randy and Laurie Spencer,
the children of my youth, the joy of my middle years.

Great Spirit . . . Listen to a grateful heart.

Turtle
Woman
Singing

7

Introduction

I believe *Who Speaks for Wolf* is one of those rare classics — having survived in oral form for centuries, it will continue to endure in this beautifully expressed written form. Indeed, this Learning Story speaks as clearly today as long ago when the event it relates played a part in the decision-making process of a group of Native Americans relocating their community.

Deceptively simple, the story can be read on multiple levels of understanding. Each re-reading may raise different questions or reveal new meanings. Frank Howell's art will open windows to new perceptions — art and text complementing and echoing the universal concepts present in each.

Who Speaks for Wolf is a reading out loud book — particularly to children. Finding out what questions they raise may present a new learning experience for you. And as you discover how it was for those people seeking a new home in the forest, so may you discover how it might be for your children and your children's children.

"And what may we learn from this" was the question the author's father asked each time he retold the story to her. That many more may learn is Paula Underwood Spencer's reason for writing it down. That many more may see is Frank Howell's reason for creating the art to accompany it. To encourage this visualizing, this listening, this learning is the reason the Meredith Slobod Crist Memorial Fund is publishing *Who Speaks for Wolf*.

Making this Indian Learning Story available is the Fund's first major service to the public. Before establishing the Fund in 1982, I had thought of this story as a logical first step in introducing Paula's historical work now in preparation. To publish "Who Speaks for Wolf" now as a memorial to my daughter, Meredith, has tempered with great poignancy my

9

happiness in bringing together the many resources needed to produce this beautiful book.

Besides the ancient vibrations felt in text and art, much love is present in this particular volume. Author and artist contributed the use of their word pictures and visual conceptions. Caught up in the project Bob Helberg worked long hours beyond his original commitment as design and production manager. Production costs were a contribution from the Overseas Education Fund through funds given to them in honor of Meredith. The Meredith Slobod Crist Memorial Fund provided the mechanism for publishing and distributing, with all proceeds from this edition to go for charitable and educational purposes. And as parents of Meredith, my husband and I worked on this memorial with great love for her. We believe, as she did, this ancient story will provide a focal point for much future learning, leading to understanding, and resulting in wisdom.

Jeanne Lamar Slobod, President
The Meredith Slobod Crist Memorial Fund
June 8, 1983

Who Speaks for Wolf

12

Who Speaks for Wolf

Almost at the edge of the circle of light cast by Central Fire — Wolf was standing. His eyes reflected the fire's warmth with a colder light. Wolf stood there, staring at the fire.

13

A boy of eight winters was watching Wolf — as immobile as Wolf — as fascinated. Finally, the boy turned to Grandfather, warming his old bones from winter's first chill.

"Why does Wolf stand there and only watch the fire?"

"Why do you?" Grandfather replied.

And then the boy remembered that he had sat there, ever since the fire was lit, watching the flames — until Wolf came. Now, instead, he watched Wolf. He saw that it was because Wolf was so different from him, yet also watched the fire, and that there seemed no fear in Wolf. It was this the boy did not understand.

Beyond where Wolf was standing there was a hill — still so close to the Central Fire that the boy was surprised to see the dim outline of another Wolf face. This one was looking at the moon.

14

Moon-Looking-Wolf began to sing her song. More and more joined her until at last even Wolf-Looks-at-Fire chortled in his throat the beginnings of a song. They sang for the Moon, and for each other, and for any who might listen. They sang of how Earth was a good place to be, of how much beauty surrounds us, and of how all this is sometimes most easily seen in Moon and Fire.

The boy listened — and wanted to do nothing else with his life but listen to Wolf singing.

After a long and particularly beautiful song, Moon-Looking-Wolf quieted, and one by one her brothers joined her in silence, until even the most distant — crying ''I am here! Don't forget me!'' — made space for the night and watched — and waited. Wolf-Looks-at-Fire turned and left the clearing, joining his brothers near the hill.

But I still don't understand," the boy continued. "Why does Wolf look at Fire? Why does he feel at home so close to our living space? Why does Wolf Woman begin her song on a hill so close to us who are not Wolf?"

"We have known each other for a long time," the old man answered. "We have learned to live with one another."

The boy still looked puzzled. Within himself he saw only the edges of understanding.

Grandfather was silent for a time — and then began at last the slow cadences of a chant. The boy knew with satisfaction that soon he would understand — would know Wolf better than before — would learn how it had been between us.

LONG AGO . . . LONG AGO . . . LONG AGO

. . . Grandfather chanted, the rhythm taking its place with
Wolf's song as something appropriate for the forest,

LONG AGO
   Our People grew in number so that where we were
      was no longer enough
   Many young men
      were sent out from among us
         to seek a new place
            where the People might be who-they-were
   They searched
      and they returned
         each with a place selected
         each determined his place was best

AND SO IT WAS
   That the People had a decision to make:
      which of the many was most appropriate

17

NOW, AT THAT TIME
   There was one among the People
      to whom Wolf was brother
   He was so much Wolf's brother
      that he would sing their song to them
         and they would answer him
   He was so much Wolf's brother
      that their young
         would sometimes follow him through the forest
         and it seemed they meant to learn from him

SO IT WAS, AT THIS TIME
   That the People gave That One a special name
   They called him WOLF'S BROTHER
      and if any sought to learn about Wolf
      if any were curious
         or wanted to learn to sing Wolf's song
            they would sit beside him
               and describe their curiosity
                  hoping for a reply

"Has it been since that time that we sing to Wolf?" the boy asked eagerly. "Was it he who taught us how?" He clapped his hand over his mouth to stop the tumble of words. He knew he had interrupted Grandfather's Song.

The old man smiled, and the crinkles around his eyes spoke of other boys — and other times.

"Yes, even he!" he answered. "For since that time it has pleased many of our people to sing to Wolf and to learn to understand him."

Encouraged, the boy asked, "And ever since our hunters go to learn to sing to Wolf?"

20

"Many people go, not only hunters. Many people go, not only men," Grandfather chided. "For was it not Wolf Woman who began the song tonight? Would it then be appropriate if only the men among us replied?"

The boy looked crestfallen. He wanted so much to be a hunter — to learn Wolf's song, but he knew there was wisdom in Grandfather's words. Not only hunters learn from Wolf.

"But you have led me down a different path," the Old One was saying. "It would please me to finish my first song."

The boy settled back and waited to learn.

AS I HAVE SAID
   The People sought a new place in the forest
   They listened closely to each of the young men
      as they spoke of hills and trees
         of clearings and running water
         of deer and squirrel and berries
   They listened to hear which place
      might be drier in rain
      more protected in winter
      and where our Three Sisters
         Corn, Beans, and Squash
            might find a place to their liking
   They listened
      and they chose

Before they chose
  they listened to each young man
Before they chose
  they listened to each among them
    he who understood the flow of waters
    she who understood Long House construction
    he who understood the storms of winter
    she who understood Three Sisters
  to each of these they listened
    until they reached agreement
    and the Eldest among them
      finally rose and said:
      "SO BE IT —
        FOR SO IT IS"

23

"BUT WAIT"
  Someone cautioned —
    "Where is Wolf's Brother?
      WHO, THEN, SPEAKS FOR WOLF?"

BUT
  THE PEOPLE WERE DECIDED
    and their mind was firm
    and the first people were sent
      to choose a site for the first Long House
      to clear a space for our Three Sisters
      to mold the land so that water
        would run away from our dwelling
          so that all would be secure within

AND THEN WOLF'S BROTHER RETURNED
    He asked about the New Place
        and said at once that we must choose another
        "You have chosen the Center Place
            for a great community of Wolf"
    But we answered him
        that many had already gone
        and that it could not wisely be changed
        and that surely Wolf could make way for us
            as we sometimes make way for Wolf
    But Wolf's Brother counseled —
        "I think that you will find
            that it is too small a place for both
            and that it will require more work then —
                than change would presently require"

BUT
    THE PEOPLE CLOSED THEIR EARS
        and would not reconsider
    When the New Place was ready
        all the People rose up as one
            and took those things they found of value
            and looked at last upon their new home   25

NOW CONSIDER HOW IT WAS FOR THEM
   This New Place
      had cool summers and winter protection
      and fast-moving streams
      and forests around us
         filled with deer and squirrel
      there was room even for our Three Beloved Sisters

AND THE PEOPLE SAW THAT THIS WAS GOOD
   AND DID NOT SEE
      WOLF WATCHING FROM THE SHADOWS!

BUT AS TIME PASSED
   They began to see —
      for someone would bring deer or squirrel
         and hang him from a tree
         and go for something to contain the meat
         but would return
            to find nothing hanging from the tree
            AND WOLF BEYOND

AT FIRST
   This seemed to us an appropriate exchange —
      some food for a place to live

27

BUT
    It soon became apparent that it was more than this —
        for Wolf would sometimes walk between the dwellings
            that we had fashioned for ourselves
                and the women grew concerned
                    for the safety of the little ones
  Thinking of this
        they devised for awhile an agreement with Wolf
            whereby the women would gather together
                at the edge of our village
                and put out food for Wolf and his brothers

BUT IT WAS SOON APPARENT
  That this meant too much food
    and also Wolf grew bolder
      coming in to look for food
        so that it was worse than before
WE HAD NO WISH TO TAME WOLF

AND SO
  Hearing the wailing of the women
    the men devised a system
      whereby some ones among them
        were always alert to drive off Wolf

28

AND WOLF WAS SOON HIS OLD UNTAMED SELF

BUT
   They soon discovered
      that this required so much energy
         that there was little left for winter preparations
        and the Long Cold began to look longer and colder
           with each passing day

29

THEN
   The men counseled together
      to choose a different course

THEY SAW
   That neither providing Wolf with food
      nor driving him off
         gave the People a life that was pleasing

THEY SAW
   That Wolf and the People
      could not live comfortably together
         in such a small space

THEY SAW
   That it was possible
      to hunt down this Wolf People
         until they were no more

30

BUT THEY ALSO SAW
   That this would require much energy over many years

THEY SAW, TOO,
   That such a task would change the People:
      they would become Wolf Killers
   A People who took life only to sustain their own
      would become a People who took life
         rather than move a little

IT DID NOT SEEM TO THEM
   THAT THEY WANTED TO BECOME SUCH A PEOPLE

AT LAST
   One of the Eldest of the People
      spoke what was in every mind:
      "It would seem
         that Wolf's Brother's vision
            was sharper than our own
   To live here indeed requires more work now
      than change would have made necessary"

32

Grandfather paused, making his knee a drum on which to maintain the rhythm of the chant, and then went on.

NOW THIS WOULD BE A SIMPLE TELLING
OF A PEOPLE WHO DECIDED TO MOVE
ONCE WINTER WAS PAST

EXCEPT
THAT FROM THIS
THE PEOPLE LEARNED A GREAT LESSON

IT IS A LESSON
we have never forgotten

33

FOR
   At the end of their Council
     one of the Eldest rose again and said:
      "Let us learn from this
        so that not again
          need the People build only to move
        Let us not again think we will gain energy
          only to lose more than we gain
        We have learned to choose a place
          where winter storms are less
            rather than rebuild
        We have learned to choose a place
          where water does not stand
            rather than sustain sickness

      LET US NOW LEARN TO CONSIDER WOLF!"

AND SO IT WAS
   That the People devised among themselves
      a way of asking each other questions
         whenever a decision was to be made
            on a New Place or a New Way
   We sought to perceive the flow of energy
      through each new possibility
         and how much was enough
         and how much was too much

UNTIL AT LAST
   Someone would rise
      and ask the old, old question
         to remind us of things
            we do not yet see clearly enough to remember

"TELL ME NOW MY BROTHERS
TELL ME NOW MY SISTERS
WHO SPEAKS FOR WOLF?"

And so Grandfather's Song ended . . . and my father's voice grew still.

"Did the boy learn to sing with Wolf?" I asked.

"All may," my father answered.

"And did the People always remember to ask Wolf's Question?"

My father smiled. "They remembered for a long time . . . a long time. And when the wooden ships came, bringing a new People, they looked at them and saw that what we accomplish by much thought and considering the needs of all, they accomplish by building tools and changing the Earth, with much thought of winter and little of tomorrow. We could not teach them to ask Wolf's question. They did not understand he was their brother. We knew how long it had taken us to listen to Wolf's voice. It seemed to us that These Ones could also learn. And so we cherished them . . . when we could . . . and held them off . . . when we must . . . and gave them time to learn."

"Will they learn, do you think, my father? Will they learn?"

"Sometimes wisdom comes only after great foolishness. We still hope they will learn. I do not know even if

our own People still ask their question. I only know that at the last Great Council when we talked about the Small Ones in their wooden ships and decided that their way and our way might exist side by side — and decided, therefore, to let them live . . . I only know that someone rose to remind them of the things we had not yet learned about these Pale Ones.''

"He rose and he reminded us of what we had already learned, of how these New Ones believed that only one way was Right and all others Wrong. He wondered out loud whether they would be as patient with us — once they were strong — as we were now with them. He wondered what else might be true for them that we did not yet see. He wondered how all these things — seen and unseen — might affect our lives and the lives of our children's children's children. Then to remind us of the great difficulties that may arise from the simple omission of something we forgot to consider, he gazed slowly around the Council Circle and asked the ancient question:

"TELL ME NOW MY BROTHERS
TELL ME NOW MY SISTERS
WHO SPEAKS FOR WOLF?"

The Author: Paula Underwood Spencer

Turtle Woman Singing

"You are Indian," her father told her, "and Irish and English and Welsh. Scots on your mother's side. So many people from whom to learn."

Yet her favorite learnings always were the ancient songs he would only sing when seated on the earth; "to remind us of our unity," he said.

This awareness of life as a whole process, of earth as a unity, led Paula through the long hours of learning, of memorization, and on to Western study, a career in international affairs.

"The Iroquois always were concerned with how a People govern themselves," her father said. And so she earned a Master's from George Washington University, studied economics and law, communications and organization; understood it all as relating to such Learning Stories as "Who Speaks for Wolf."

Paula worked for the Senate Foreign Relations Subcommittee on Disarmament, knowing such people as Hubert Humphrey, and understanding their contributions. She was Foreign Affairs Assistant to Robert R. Barry, a member of the House Foreign Affairs Committee, while the Peace Corps was formed. As her children grew, she joined the League of Women Voters, understanding in advance the nature of consensus, the Central Fire that lights a People's Way.

For twelve years she worked for the Overseas Education Fund, six of those years as vice president for the Asian Program, focusing on how a People — any people — organize themselves, and decide.

Born bi-cultural, she studied cross-cultural relations, taking no small joy in this growing Western awareness. During her lifetime she has watched an amazing cultural myopia slowly turn toward perceived complexity: more confusing, . . more accurate.

Now, after fifty years of learning, Paula begins the task of recreating all she learned from her father; all he learned from his; all her great-great grandmother had preserved so that it might one day be given to all Earth's children.

43

The Artist: Frank Howell

Of himself, Frank Howell says: "If you want to know me, know my work."

Author Paula Spencer says of Frank: "Through the medium of his art, he shows the complex workings of the human spirit. That his form of expression speaks in Native American terms hardly matters. What Frank is saying transcends any one approach to life. But for those with any feeling for that which is called Indian, his work contains a special wonder."

Frank is most widely known for his Indian imagery which was greatly influenced by a period of his life spent in Taos, N.M. He says: "The Indian is the vehicle to express my feelings. I find myself in harmony with Indian philosophy. They are a people with an extraordinary will to survive."

Frank executes his work with a degree of excellence and dignity reminiscent of the Old Masters, with an absolute control of drawing, form and design. He works fluidly in many media including acrylic, watercolor, oil, graphite and ink as well as being accomplished in the art of lithography.

An Iowa native, Frank Howell graduated from the University of Northern Iowa in 1960, and continued his graduate work in creative writing and poetry. During this time, he taught art on both high school and college levels, and went on to establish studios in Breckenridge, Co. and Taos, N.M. He currently maintains a studio and print atelier in Englewood, Colorado.

Frank has had over forty one-man exhibitions and his work has been shown at university, museum, and private galleries, as well as hanging in many private and corporate collections. Recently, a major Frank Howell painting was purchased by the Shelburne Museum in Vermont, and he has completed several important commissions for Execucom Corporation, Austin, Texas; City Center Four Office Complex, Denver; KRMA Public Television Station, Denver; and an important series of 25 drawings for Art Associates of Colorado.

As well as being a multi-faceted and talented visual artist, Frank has had several publications and published articles which reflect his talents in poetry and writing. He is currently working on books combining his paintings with his writing.

44

"Preservation of an Oral History Of Pre-Oneida People"

When an oral history turns out to be one that has miraculously survived for over ten thousand years, it ceases to be a prosaic task of recording and turns into an exciting and significant event. Although Paula Underwood Spencer makes no claim other than she is recording accurately the "songs her father sang," she feels and believes the authenticity behind his words. She is aware of the sacrifices made by her ancestors and of the dedication despite great difficulties they devoted to perpetuating this history.

Much of what is in the literature about our early Native Americans is told from the White Man's point of view, missing some things and adding others. Indians sometimes told early explorers, and later anthropologists, what they felt these people wanted to hear, avoiding subjects they found Westerners unprepared to accept. In general, Indians became wary of sharing important or sacred information with outsiders, finding so often misunderstanding or a lack of respect. But Paula accepted from her ancestors a charge to preserve their history for *all* people.

Paula's great-great grandmother, Tsilikomah, left her Oneida home long before the Western process of tribal registration began, her descendants also living apart from other Iroquois. Paula and her father became a "Tribe of Two" as they followed the ancient Indian traditions. Paula feels herself a bridge between Western and Indian cultures: educated by her father as a strong spirit person, she also went through the public school and university systems, and lived, on the surface, a seemingly typical Western life.

Tsilikomah, *Keeper of the Old Things* for her Oneida community, fled from her home around 1800 when that Oneida Council decided to sacrifice their ancient Tellings and possessions. She felt strongly her responsibility to go where it would be possible to preserve the stories so painstakingly treasured over thousands of years. Finding refuge with Quaker friends, she then lived in hiding from all Iroquois. Against difficulties she survived to pass her oral history and Learning Stories on to her grandson, Oliver Perry Underwood (Grey Wolf Walking).

45

Oliver passed the stories and spirit training on to his son, Perry Leonard Underwood (Sharp-eyed Hawk). Although dyslectic, Leonard's conceptual and memorization skills and his abilities in the ancient Oneida and hand languages were exceptional. Using these traditional Indian learning techniques and spirit structures, Leonard transmitted the stories to his daughter, Paula. Paula accepted the mission to set the Tellings down in English when she reached fifty. This timing was arranged so she might lead a normal life and in the expectation that time would bring a more favorable Western attitude toward Indian perceptions.

Paula turned fifty in 1982 and has begun her task. She expects to publish the Tellings under the title "The Walking People." She is writing down the Learning Stories her father used with her as a specific learning technique — the first of these being "Who Speaks for Wolf." Details of childhood experiences resulting from her commitment to learning this vast history will be gathered together under the title, "A Tribe of Two." "Standing in the Middle of a Memory" will recount the methods she must use to reconstruct the materials stored in her memory. The entire project may take as long as five years to write, but each year will see the completion of various segments.

The Tellings recount the travels and trials of one small group of human beings as they leave their home where they had lived "So Long No One Any Longer Remembers How Long" to migrate across "Walk by Waters" to the "Great Island that Lies Beyond." Because of their constant search for information and knowledge, they also recount what they learned from various peoples along the way.

The stories show this group's power of decision making, their abilities to reason and to organize themselves both for survival and ease of living as they leave Asia to cross the Bering Strait and finally arrive in the Great Lakes region where their descendants became known as the Oneida — one of the six nations of the Iroquois Confederacy. The Tellings will provide a glimpse into the beginnings of organizational and governmental procedures which developed into the Iroquois Confederation which, in turn, influenced the direction of our own form of democracy and Constitution. The influence of Iroquois statesmen on our founding fathers, such as Benjamin Franklin and Thomas Jefferson has been documented. Paula's stories substantiate this but present it from an Iroquois point of view.

Paula's memory may be the sole remaining source of some of this material. Hence, the importance of enabling her to take the necessary time to record it. The Fund is proud of its first project and the role it has played in encouraging Paula in this important work.

The Meredith Slobod Crist Memorial Fund

Established in 1982 to celebrate the unique life of Meredith, this Fund commemorates the extraordinary impact she had upon many individuals. The Fund is designed to carry on projects of significance which, through channeling special talents and abilities into constructive goals, will enable individuals — especially women — to make a difference in their own lives and to society.

The Fund has already helped support publication of a handbook "Women Working Together for Personal, Economic and Community Development" published by the Overseas Education Fund in Washington, D.C. to be used by them in working toward their goal to improve the economic conditions of Third World women and their families. The Fund is also providing seed money for the Women and World Issues group in Austin, Texas, to plan and put on a workshop.

Designated as a publicly-supported organization, the Fund is exempt for Federal income tax purposes under Section 501 (c)(3). It solicits funds from individuals, corporations, and organizations for monies to carry out its purpose. Publishing this memorial volume is not only the Fund's first major service to the public and a fundraiser for the purposes of the Fund, but it is also part of a major commitment to the first project it has selected to support: "Preservation of an Oral History of Pre-Oneida People."

This delicate strength,
With the breath
Of an almost invisible wind,
Lifts Eagle
Far beyond sight.

August 1983
Paula Underwood Spencer